I0019063

E-Memories: Crafting a Personal Narrative in the Digital Space

Hiroko Oe

Table Of Contents

01

Chapter 1: Embracing the Digital Landscape

Understanding the Shift in Storytelling

The landscape of storytelling has undergone a profound transformation in the digital age, inviting new voices and perspectives into the narrative fold. With the advent of social media platforms, blogs, and various digital tools, anyone with a story to tell can now reach an audience far beyond their immediate circle. This shift not only democratizes storytelling but also enriches it, allowing for a diverse range of experiences and insights to be shared. As digital fans and storytelling lovers, you have the opportunity to explore this vibrant landscape and contribute your unique narrative to the collective tapestry of human experience.

In this new era, the way we engage with our memories has changed dramatically. Traditional memoir writing often focused on a linear narrative, but digital storytelling embraces a more fluid approach. You can weave together images, videos, and text to create a multifaceted representation of your experiences. This multimedia aspect allows for a richer exploration of your memories, as you can capture the emotions and nuances of your story in ways that text alone may not convey. Embrace these tools and experiment with different formats to find the most authentic expression of your narrative.

Moreover, the digital space fosters a sense of community that can enhance your storytelling journey. Online platforms provide a space for connection and collaboration, where you can share your memoirs and receive feedback from fellow storytellers. Engaging with an audience can inspire you to delve deeper into your memories and refine your narrative. The interactive nature of digital storytelling encourages dialogue, allowing you to not only share your experiences but also learn from others. This exchange can be incredibly enriching, as it broadens your perspective and helps you appreciate the myriad ways in which stories can be told.

As you navigate this new storytelling landscape, it's essential to recognize the importance of authenticity. In a world saturated with curated images and polished narratives, your genuine voice stands out. Don't be afraid to share the messy, imperfect parts of your story; these moments often resonate most deeply with others. Embrace vulnerability, and let your true self shine through your writing. This authenticity invites connection and relatability, allowing others to see themselves in your experiences and fostering a sense of belonging in the digital community.

Ultimately, understanding the shift in storytelling empowers you to embrace your role as a digital memoirist. Your memories are valuable, and sharing them online can create a legacy that extends beyond your lifetime. With an encouraging spirit and an openness to new forms of expression, you can craft a personal narrative that not only honors your journey but also inspires others. As you embark on this exciting adventure, remember that your story matters, and the digital space is waiting for your unique voice to emerge.

Opportunities for Digital Memoirists

The digital age has transformed the way we think about memoir writing, opening doors to new possibilities for those who wish to share their personal stories. As a digital memoirist, you have the unique opportunity to harness technology to create rich, engaging narratives that resonate with audiences far and wide. This landscape is not just about putting pen to paper or fingers to keyboard; it's about exploring multimedia formats, interactive storytelling, and building communities around shared experiences. The digital realm invites you to innovate and express your true self in ways that were once unimaginable.

One of the most significant opportunities for digital memoirists lies in the accessibility of platforms that allow for creative expression. From blogs to social media, you can easily share snippets of your life with a global audience. This democratized space encourages you to experiment with various formats—be it written word, video, or audio—allowing you to choose the medium that best reflects your voice. The flexibility of these platforms means you can adapt your storytelling style over time, learning from your audience and refining your craft as you go along.

Moreover, the digital landscape fosters connection and community. By sharing your memoir online, you invite others to engage with your story, creating a dialogue around your experiences. Readers can comment, share, and even contribute their own narratives, enriching the conversation and expanding the context of your memoir. This interaction not only validates your voice but also builds a network of support among fellow storytellers and fans. Engaging with your audience can lead to collaborative opportunities, such as joint projects or even workshops, further enhancing your skills as a digital memoirist.

In addition to connecting with readers, digital memoirists have the chance to tap into a wealth of resources and tools that can aid in the writing process. From writing apps that help you structure your narrative to platforms that offer guidance on digital marketing, the resources available are vast and varied. Embracing these tools can enhance your storytelling capabilities and help you reach a wider audience. The ability to analyze data and feedback allows you to refine your approach, ensuring that your memoir resonates with those who matter most: your readers.

Ultimately, the opportunities for digital memoirists are boundless, encouraging you to embrace your unique story and share it with the world. This era offers a platform for self-expression that is both powerful and liberating. By weaving your personal narrative into the digital fabric of our time, you contribute to a rich tapestry of diverse voices and experiences. So take heart, embrace the journey, and let your digital memoir shine brightly in the vast expanse of online storytelling.

The Power of Personal Narratives Online

In the digital age, personal narratives have evolved into powerful tools for connection and expression. The internet provides an expansive platform where individuals can share their life stories, experiences, and reflections, reaching audiences far beyond their immediate circles. By crafting and sharing personal narratives online, individuals not only document their own journeys but also contribute to the rich tapestry of human experience. This communal storytelling fosters empathy, understanding, and a sense of belonging, encouraging each storyteller to embrace their unique voice.

Sharing personal narratives online can be a transformative experience. It empowers individuals to reflect on their lives, recognize their growth, and articulate their emotions in a meaningful way. When people recount their stories, they often uncover insights about themselves that may have remained hidden. This self-discovery can be liberating, enabling them to embrace their past while shaping their future. The act of writing and sharing becomes a cathartic process, allowing individuals to connect with their inner selves and, in turn, invite others to connect with them.

The digital landscape amplifies the reach of these personal narratives, allowing stories to transcend geographical boundaries. Memorable experiences can resonate with diverse audiences, inspiring others facing similar challenges or celebrating triumphs. As readers engage with these stories, they may find solace, encouragement, or motivation in the shared human experience. The power of personal narratives lies not only in their ability to connect people but also in their capacity to spark conversations and foster community among those who might otherwise feel isolated in their experiences.

Moreover, the online realm offers various formats for storytelling, from blogs and social media posts to podcasts and video blogs. This diversity allows individuals to express themselves in ways that feel authentic and comfortable. Whether you prefer writing, speaking, or creating visual content, there is a platform suited to your style. Experimenting with different formats can enhance your storytelling skills and help you find the most effective way to convey your message, making your narrative all the more impactful.

Embracing the power of personal narratives online is not just about sharing stories; it is about creating a legacy. By documenting your experiences, you contribute to the collective memory that shapes our understanding of the world. Each narrative adds a unique thread to the broader story of humanity. As you embark on your journey of crafting and sharing your personal narrative, remember that your voice matters. Your story has the potential to inspire, heal, and connect with others in profound ways, making your mark in the digital landscape.

02

Chapter 2: Finding Your Voice

Discovering Your Unique Story

Discovering your unique story is an empowering journey that invites you to explore the depths of your experiences, emotions, and insights. In a world increasingly dominated by digital narratives, the importance of personal storytelling has never been more pronounced. Each of us holds a treasure trove of memories that shape who we are, and these memories can become the foundation of a compelling digital memoir. By delving into your past, you not only honor your own journey but also create a connection with others who may resonate with your experiences.

To begin this exploration, take a moment to reflect on the significant moments that have shaped your life. Consider the milestones, challenges, and triumphs that have defined your path. These moments, both big and small, weave together to form the tapestry of your identity. As you jot down these memories, allow yourself to feel the emotions attached to them. What lessons did you learn? How did these experiences influence your choices? This process of introspection is crucial in uncovering the themes and threads that will ultimately define your unique story.

Once you have identified key moments, think about the perspectives that make your narrative distinctive. Your voice is a powerful tool in storytelling, and it reflects your individual worldview. Embrace your unique style, whether it's humorous, poignant, or reflective. As you write, let your personality shine through. Remember, authenticity resonates with readers; they are drawn to genuine voices that convey real experiences. The digital space offers endless possibilities for sharing your narrative, so don't shy away from experimenting with different formats, such as blogs, social media posts, or multimedia presentations.

As you craft your memoir, consider the impact of your story on your audience. Your experiences may mirror those of others, providing comfort, inspiration, or even a sense of belonging. By sharing your journey, you open the door for dialogue and connection. Allow yourself to be vulnerable, as it is often in our rawness that we find strength. Engage with your readers through comments or feedback, and be open to the conversations that emerge from your storytelling. This interaction not only enriches your narrative but also builds a community around shared experiences.

Finally, remember that discovering your unique story is an ongoing process. Your narrative will evolve as you continue to grow and experience life. Embrace the idea that your memoir can be a living document, reflecting the changes and insights you gain over time. As you share your story in the digital space, you contribute to a collective tapestry of human experience. Each narrative adds depth to the larger picture, reminding us all of our interconnectedness. Celebrate your unique journey, and let it inspire others to uncover their stories as well.

The Importance of Authenticity

In a world overflowing with curated images and polished narratives, the importance of authenticity in storytelling cannot be overstated. When you share your personal experiences online, you have the unique opportunity to connect with others on a deeper level. Authenticity allows you to strip away the layers of perfection that often shroud our lives and instead present a genuine representation of who you are. This raw honesty resonates with readers, fostering relationships built on trust and understanding. Embracing your true self in your e-memories not only enriches your narrative but also encourages others to be authentic in their own storytelling journeys.

Writing an authentic memoir in the digital space invites you to explore the nuances of your experiences. It encourages reflection on both the joyful and challenging moments that shape your life. As you delve into your memories, consider how these experiences have molded your identity. Sharing the highs and lows not only humanizes your story but also makes it relatable to others who may have faced similar situations. By being honest about your struggles, triumphs, and everything in between, you weave a narrative that speaks to the heart, inspiring readers to reflect on their own journeys.

Moreover, authenticity in your e-memories fosters a sense of belonging among your audience. When you share stories that are true to your identity, you invite others to engage with your narrative on a personal level. Digital fans and fellow storytelling lovers seek connections, and your willingness to be vulnerable can create a community of support and understanding. This shared experience can transform solitary memories into collective narratives, bridging gaps between diverse individuals. Through your authentic voice, you can cultivate a space where readers feel encouraged to share their own stories, creating a tapestry of interconnected experiences.

In the digital age, the challenge is often to remain true to oneself amidst the pressures of social media and online personas. It's easy to fall into the trap of comparison, believing that your story must match the glamour of others. However, embracing authenticity means recognizing the value of your unique perspective. Your journey is unlike anyone else's, and that individuality is what makes your narrative compelling. Remember that your voice matters, and it deserves to be heard without the filter of societal expectations. By showcasing your true self, you not only honor your own story but also empower others to do the same.

Ultimately, the importance of authenticity in crafting your e-memories lies in its power to inspire and uplift. By sharing your unvarnished truth, you contribute to a culture that celebrates realness over perfection. Your stories can spark conversations, foster empathy, and create lasting connections with your audience. As you embark on your memoir writing journey in the digital age, let your authenticity shine through. Celebrate your uniqueness, embrace your narrative, and inspire others to share their own e-memories with the same courage and honesty that you embody.

Techniques to Enhance Your Narrative Voice

To enhance your narrative voice in the digital landscape, it is essential to embrace authenticity. Your unique experiences and perspectives are what set your story apart, making it relatable and engaging for readers. Start by reflecting on your personal history, the emotions tied to those memories, and the lessons you've learned. This introspection will help you connect deeply with your audience, allowing them to see the world through your eyes. Write as if you are conversing with a friend, using a tone that is both inviting and open. When readers feel your sincerity, they are more likely to invest themselves in your story.

Another effective technique is to incorporate sensory details that transport your audience into your narrative. Describe the sights, sounds, smells, and feelings associated with your memories to create vivid imagery. This approach not only captivates readers but also evokes emotions that resonate with them. For instance, if you're recounting a family gathering, mention the aromas of the food, the laughter filling the air, and the warmth of shared moments. By painting a rich picture, you enable your readers to experience your memories as if they were there, fostering a deeper connection to your narrative.

Utilizing dialogue can also significantly enhance your narrative voice. Conversations bring your characters to life, allowing readers to hear their voices and understand their personalities. Including snippets of real dialogues can make your stories feel more dynamic and relatable. Don't shy away from the imperfections of speech—pauses, interruptions, and even silences can convey as much meaning as well-structured sentences. By weaving dialogue into your narrative, you create a multi-dimensional experience that invites readers to engage with your story on a personal level.

Experimenting with structure and style is another valuable technique. The digital space offers a plethora of formats to choose from, whether it's a blog post, a video, or an interactive timeline. Each medium has its own strengths, and you can play with these to enhance your narrative voice. Consider using lists, bullet points, or even multimedia elements like images and videos to complement your writing. This variety not only keeps your content fresh and exciting but also allows you to express your voice in ways that align with your storytelling goals.

Lastly, don't underestimate the power of community feedback. Sharing your drafts with friends, family, or fellow writers can provide invaluable insights into how your narrative voice resonates with others. Be open to constructive criticism and take note of what aspects of your voice shine through and what may need refinement. Engaging with a community of digital storytellers can inspire you and spark new ideas, helping you evolve your voice continuously. Remember, your narrative is a living entity, and with each revision and new piece, you have the opportunity to enhance it further.

Ø3

Chapter 3: Tools of the Trade

Choosing the Right Platforms

Choosing the right platforms for sharing your personal narrative is a pivotal step in the journey of crafting your e-memories. The digital landscape is vast, filled with opportunities to express your story in ways that resonate with both you and your audience. Whether you prefer blogging, social media, or multimedia presentations, identifying the platforms that best suit your style and content is essential. Embrace the variety available and explore each option, as each platform has unique features that can enhance your storytelling experience.

Blogs offer a timeless space for reflection and elaboration. They allow you the freedom to delve into your memories with depth and detail, creating a rich tapestry of your experiences. Platforms like WordPress or Medium provide user-friendly interfaces that enable you to customize your layout, add images, and even include audio or video clips. This flexibility invites you to engage your readers more intimately, encouraging them to connect with your narrative on a personal level. Don't hesitate to experiment with different formats to find what feels authentic to you.

Social media can be a powerful ally in sharing snippets of your journey. Platforms like Instagram and Facebook allow you to reach a broader audience quickly. With the ability to share images and short texts, you can capture moments from your life that might not require extensive elaboration but still hold significant meaning. Engaging with your followers through comments and direct messages can foster a sense of community, making your storytelling a shared experience. Consider using hashtags or participating in storytelling challenges to further expand your reach and connect with fellow digital fans.

Multimedia platforms like YouTube or podcasts present exciting opportunities to diversify your narrative. If you enjoy speaking or visual storytelling, these channels can bring your memories to life in a dynamic way. You can share your experiences through vlogs or audio stories, adding layers of emotion and personality that written words sometimes struggle to convey. The key is to find a medium that excites you, as your enthusiasm will translate into compelling content that captivates your audience.

As you navigate the selection process, remember that the right platform for you is one that aligns with your vision and storytelling style. Take the time to experiment with different mediums, and don't be afraid to combine them. Your journey in crafting e-memories is unique, and by embracing the platforms that resonate with you, you'll be well on your way to creating a captivating personal narrative that not only preserves your memories but also inspires others. Trust in your voice and the power of digital storytelling, and let your memories shine.

Digital Tools for Writing and Editing

In today's digital age, writing and editing have transformed into dynamic processes enriched by a variety of tools designed to enhance creativity and streamline workflows. For those who are passionate about storytelling and preserving memories, these digital resources can elevate your narrative craft, making it easier than ever to capture the essence of your experiences. Embracing these tools not only simplifies the writing process but also opens up new avenues for expression and connection with your audience.

One popular category of digital writing tools includes word processors and specialized software that facilitate the writing process. Applications like Google Docs and Microsoft Word provide user-friendly interfaces, enabling writers to focus on their narratives without the distraction of formatting issues. Additionally, these platforms often feature collaborati e options, allowing multiple contributors to share and refine their stories in real-time. This can be particularly beneficial for memoir writing, as it encourages feedback and support from peers who understand the emotional weight of your memories.

Editing is equally crucial in crafting a compelling personal narrative, and various digital tools can assist in this area as well. Grammar checkers like Grammarly or Hemingway Editor offer real-time suggestions to improve clarity and style. These tools can catch common mistakes and provide insights into your writing's readability, helping you communicate your thoughts more effectively. With the assistance of these digital editors, you can refine your voice and ensure that your memoir resonates with readers, allowing your unique experiences to shine through.

Moreover, digital platforms for storytelling often come with features that enhance engagement and creativity. For instance, tools like Canva enable writers to create visually appealing layouts for their memoirs, integrating images and design elements that complement their narratives. This visual storytelling aspect can captivate readers, drawing them into your memories in a more immersive way. By utilizing these resources, you can transform your written words into a rich tapestry of experiences that invites others to share in your journey.

As you embark on your memoir writing adventure in the digital space, remember that the right tools can empower you to tell your story with authenticity and flair. Embrace the technology at your fingertips, and don't hesitate to experiment with different applications and platforms. The digital landscape is vast and full of possibilities, providing you with the means to craft a personal narrative that not only preserves your memories but also inspires others to reflect on their own stories. Your journey is unique, and with the help of these digital tools, you can share it with the world in a truly impactful way.

Enhancing Your Memoir with Multimedia

In the age of technology, enhancing your memoir with multimedia elements can transform your narrative into a vibrant experience that resonates deeply with readers. By incorporating images, audio, and video, you create a dynamic storytelling platform that captivates and engages your audience. This combination allows you to convey emotions and experiences in ways that words alone may not fully capture. Imagine a cherished photograph of a family gathering paired with a voice recording of your thoughts during that moment; together, they paint a richer picture of your life story.

Multimedia allows for a more profound connection with your audience. When readers can see your smiling face in a childhood photo or hear the laughter of loved ones in a video clip, they are more likely to feel a personal connection to your story. These elements serve not just as embellishments but as essential components that enhance the emotional depth of your memoir. By sharing your experiences through various formats, you invite readers to step into your world and experience your journey alongside you, fostering empathy and understanding.

Incorporating multimedia into your memoir also opens up creative avenues for storytelling. You can experiment with formats such as interactive timelines, digital scrapbooks, or social media snapshots that highlight specific moments in your life. This creativity not only adds interest to your memoir but also allows you to express your personality and style. Think about how different media can represent different eras of your life or specific themes within your narrative. This approach not only enriches your memoir but also makes the process of creation more enjoyable and fulfilling.

Moreover, the digital landscape offers numerous tools and platforms that make integrating multimedia into your memoir easier than ever. Software and apps designed for storytelling allow you to combine text with images and audio seamlessly. You can create a blog, a website, or even a digital book that showcases your multimedia memoir in an engaging format. These platforms often come with user-friendly features that enable you to focus on your storytelling while minimizing technical challenges. Embrace these resources as you craft your narrative; they can be invaluable allies in your creative process.

Finally, remember that your memoir is a reflection of your unique voice and experiences. Multimedia should amplify your story, not overshadow it. Use these tools to complement your text, enhancing rather than distracting from your narrative. With thoughtful integration of multimedia elements, your memoir can transcend traditional boundaries, allowing you to share your memories in a way that is both authentic and impactful. Embrace the digital age and let your memories come to life through the power of multimedia storytelling.

Chapter 4: Structuring Your Memoir

Identifying Key Themes and Events

Identifying key themes and events in your life is an essential step in crafting a compelling personal narrative. As you embark on the journey of capturing your memories in the digital space, take a moment to reflect on the experiences that have shaped you. Think about the moments that made you laugh, cry, or change direction. These events, whether big or small, serve as the foundation of your story. By recognizing the themes that emerge from these experiences, you can create a narrative that resonates not only with you but also with your audience.

Begin by brainstorming significant events in your life. Consider milestones such as graduations, weddings, or career changes, but don't overlook the quieter moments that have left a lasting impact, like a conversation with a friend or a solitary walk in nature. As you list these events, ask yourself what they reveal about your values, beliefs, and identity. This process will help you uncover underlying themes, such as resilience, love, or transformation, that can weave your narrative together, making it more cohesive and engaging.

Once you've identified key events, it's time to analyze them for recurring themes. Look for patterns in your experiences that illustrate a particular aspect of your life journey. For instance, if you notice that many of your significant events center around personal growth or overcoming challenges, these can become central themes in your memoir. Themes act as guiding lights in your narrative, providing depth and context to your story. They allow rea ters to connect with your experiences on a personal level, fostering empathy and understandir.ɟ.

As you craft your narrative, consider how these themes and events can be interlinked. Create a timeline that visualizes how different experiences relate to one another. This exercise can spark inspiration for how to structure your memoir, guiding you to explore the connections between your past and present. Emphasize the lessons learned and how they have influenced your current perspective. This not only enriches your narrative but also encourages readers to reflect on their own experiences and find meaning within them.

Finally, remember that identifying key themes and events is an ongoing process. As you write and revise your narrative, new insights may emerge. Embrace this fluidity and allow your story to evolve. Your experiences and their significance can change over time, reflecting your growth and understanding. By remaining open to this evolution, you create a dynamic and relatable memoir that captures the essence of your journey in the digital age. Your story is unique, and by sharing it, you contribute to a rich tapestry of interconnected lives and experiences, inspiring others along the way.

Creating an Engaging Narrative Arc

Creating an engaging narrative arc is the backbone of any compelling story, and in the realm of digital memoir writing, this becomes even more crucial. The narrative arc serves as the roadmap for your readers, guiding them through a journey filled with emotions, revelations, and connections. As you weave your personal experiences into a cohesive story, remember that the structure of your narrative should evoke curiosity and empathy. Think about the key moments in your life that have shaped who you are today, and consider how these moments can be transformed into a captivating storyline that resonates with your audience.

To begin crafting your narrative arc, start with a strong hook. This could be an intriguing question, a vivid memory, or a striking statement that immediately draws your readers in. Your opening should set the tone for the rest of your memoir, promising a journey that is both personal and universal. As you share your experiences, think about how each element of your story connects to the larger themes you wish to explore. This connection will not only engage your readers but also provide them with a sense of purpose as they reflect on their own lives in relation to yours.

As you move through the stages of your narrative arc, consider the rise and fall of tension in your story. The moments of conflict, struggle, and resolution are what create emotional depth and keep readers invested in your journey. Don't shy away from sharing the challenges you faced; instead, embrace them as pivotal points in your narrative. Highlighting your vulnerabilities and how you overcame them can create a powerful bond with your audience, encouraging them to reflect on their own challenges and triumphs. This shared experience fosters a sense of community among readers, as they see parts of themselves in your story.

Transitioning through the climax and resolution of your narrative arc is equally important. The climax should be the most intense moment of your story, where everything you've been building toward comes to a head. This is where your readers will feel the most engaged, as they anticipate the outcome of your journey. Following this, provide a resolution that no only ties up the loose ends but also offers insight or reflection. This is your opportunity to share the lessons learned or the changes experienced as a result of your journey, leaving your readers with something to ponder long after they've finished reading.

Finally, remember that creating an engaging narrative arc is not merely about the structure but also about authenticity. Write from the heart, allowing your unique voice to shine through. The digital space offers you the chance to infuse multimedia elements into your memoir, such as photos, videos, or audio clips, which can enhance your narrative experience. By embracing these tools and remaining true to your story, you will not only engage your audience but also create a lasting impact that resonates with them. Your personal narrative is a gift to the world, and by crafting it thoughtfully, you can inspire others to reflect on their own e-memories and the stories they wish to tell.

Balancing Chronology and Theme

Balancing chronology and theme in your personal narrative is crucial for creating a compelling memoir in the digital space. While chronological storytelling provides a clear timeline that guides readers through your life events, thematic storytelling allows for deeper exploration of emotions, insights, and lessons learned. The key is to weave these two elements together, crafting a narrative that resonates with your audience on multiple levels. This approach not only enhances engagement but also enriches the reader's experience, making your memories come alive in a vibrant and relatable way.

To begin balancing these elements, consider the overarching themes you want to convey in your memoir. Identify the key messages, emotions, or experiences that have shaped your life. These themes will serve as the backbone of your narrative, allowing you to connect personal anecdotes with broader reflections. As you outline your story, think about how specific events can illustrate these themes. By doing so, you create a dynamic interplay between chronology and theme, where each moment in time serves a greater purpose in conveying your message.

As you dive into your memories, you may find it helpful to experiment with non-linear storytelling. This technique allows you to jump between different points in your life, connecting them through themes rather than strict chronology. For example, if resilience is a central theme, you might start with a moment of triumph, then flash back to earlier challenges that laid the groundwork for that success. This method not only keeps your readers intrigued but also emphasizes how experiences interconnect, revealing the progression of your personal growth in a more profound way.

In the digital age, you have the added advantage of multimedia tools at your disposal. Incorporating images, videos, or audio clips can enhance your narrative by providing visual and auditory context to key moments. Use these elements to highlight significant themes as they relate to specific memories. For instance, a photograph from a pivotal event can evoke emotions and serve as a visual anchor for your readers, reinforcing the themes you are exploring. This multi-faceted approach allows for a richer narrative experience that can resonate with diverse audiences.

Ultimately, balancing chronology and theme invites you to reflect on your journey with intention and creativity. Embrace the process of crafting your memoir by allowing both elements to inform and enrich each other. As you weave your stories together, remember that your unique perspective is what will engage and inspire your readers. By thoughtfully integrating these aspects, you create a personal narrative that not only preserves your memories but also fosters a deeper connection with those who share a passion for storytelling.

Chapter 5: The Art of Reflection

The Benefits of Reflective Writing

Reflective writing serves as a powerful tool for those looking to craft their personal narratives in the digital space. One of the most significant benefits of this practice is its ability to deepen self-awareness. When you take the time to reflect on your experiences, thoughts, and emotions, you gain insights that may have previously gone unnoticed. This heightened self-awareness not only enriches your memoir but also enhances your overall understanding of yourself, allowing you to connect more authentically with your audience.

Another important advantage of reflective writing is its role in emotional processing. Life is filled with challenges, joys, and intricate moments that can be difficult to navigate. Engaging in reflective writing gives you a safe space to unpack these emotions, offering clarity and perspective on your experiences. By articulating your feelings on the page, you can transform confusion into understanding, turning past struggles into valuable lessons that resonate with readers and inspire them to reflect on their own journeys.

Additionally, reflective writing encourages creativity. As you contemplate your experiences, you may discover new angles or themes to explore within your narrative. This creative process allows you to weave together memories in innovative ways, making your story more engaging and relatable. The act of reflection can spark inspiration and lead to unexpected revelations, which can elevate your memoir from a simple recounting of events to a compelling narrative that captures the imagination of your audience.

Moreover, reflective writing fosters a sense of connection with others. Sharing your reflections not only provides insight into your own life but also invites readers to examine their own experiences. This shared vulnerability can create a profound bond between you and your audience, making your narrative resonate on a deeper level. As you articulate your thoughts and feelings, you may find that others relate to your journey, encouraging them to share their stories in return, thus building a community of storytellers.

Finally, the practice of reflective writing serves as a valuable record of your personal growth over time. By documenting your thoughts and reflections, you create a timeline of your evolving perspectives and insights. This chronicle not only helps you track your development as a person but also enriches your memoir with layers of meaning. When you revisit your reflections, you can appreciate how far you've come, which can be both empowering and motivating as you continue to craft your narrative in the ever-expanding digital landscape.

Techniques for Deepening Your Insights

To deepen your insights as you craft your personal narrative in the digital space, consider embracing the practice of reflective journaling. This technique encourages you to regularly document your thoughts, feelings, and experiences in a dedicated digital space. By reflecting on your daily encounters, you allow your memories to surface in more vivid detail. Each entry serves as a building block for your memoir, capturing the essence of your journey. As you revisit these reflections, you'll uncover patterns and themes in your life that might have previously gone unnoticed, enriching your narrative with depth and authenticity.

Another powerful technique for enhancing your insights is the use of multimedia elements. Incorporating photos, videos, and audio recordings into your online memoir can evoke emotions and memories that text alone may not fully capture. Visual storytelling allows your audience to connect with your experiences on a deeper level. By integrating various media, you create a more immersive experience that can help you recall significant events with greater clarity. This multi-faceted approach not only engages your readers but also transforms your memories into a dynamic tapestry that reflects your unique perspective.

Engaging with a community of fellow digital storytellers can also significantly deepen your insights. By sharing your work and receiving feedback, you open yourself to different interpretations and perspectives. Online forums, writing groups, and social media platforms designed for writers can serve as invaluable resources. As you interact with others, you may discover new angles on your own experiences that you hadn't considered before. This collaborative process fosters growth and encourages you to refine your narrative, ultimately leading to a richer and more resonant memoir.

Mind mapping is another effective technique for organizing your thoughts and expanding your insights. This visual brainstorming method helps you lay out your ideas in a structured format, allowing you to explore connections between various memories and themes. By mapping out your narrative, you can identify key moments that deserve more attention or uncover hidden stories waiting to be told. This technique not only enhances your understanding of your own life story but also aids in crafting a cohesive narrative that flows seamlessly across your digital memoir.

Lastly, practice mindfulness to deepen your insights as you write. Setting aside time to be present with your thoughts can lead to profound realizations about your past experiences. Whether through meditation, quiet reflection, or simply taking a walk in nature, cultivating mindfulness helps you connect with your emotions and memories on a deeper level. This heightened awareness enriches your storytelling, allowing you to convey your experiences with sincerity and depth. By taking the time to explore your inner world, you ultimately enhance the authenticity of your memoir, creating a narrative that resonates both with you and your audience.

Incorporating Reflection into Your Memoir

Incorporating reflection into your memoir is a powerful way to deepen the reader's connection to your story. Reflection allows you to step back from the events of your life and consider their significance, offering insights that can resonate with your audience. As you craft your memoir in the digital space, think about how your experiences shaped you and what lessons you learned along the way. Your reflections can provide a bridge between your personal narrative and the collective experiences of your readers, helping them find parallels in their own lives.

Begin by identifying key moments in your story that invite reflection. These could be turning points, challenges, or moments of joy. As you revisit these memories, ask yourself what you learned from them and how they influenced your current perspective. This process of introspection not only enriches your narrative but also encourages readers to reflect on their own journeys. By sharing your thoughts and insights, you create an engaging dialogue that invites readers to think critically about their own experiences, making your memoir a shared space of growth and understanding.

When writing your reflections, aim for authenticity. Share your thoughts honestly, even if they reveal vulnerabilities or uncertainties. Readers appreciate sincerity and are more likely to connect with your story when they sense your genuine voice. Use your reflections to explore emotions, motivations, and conflicts that arose during those pivotal moments. This depth will not only enhance your memoir but also inspire readers to open up about their own feelings and experiences, fostering a sense of community around your digital narrative.

Consider incorporating multimedia elements to complement your reflections. In the digital age, storytelling is not limited to text; images, videos, and audio clips can enhance the emotional impact of your memoir. For instance, a photograph from a significant moment can evoke memories and emotions that words alone may not capture. By weaving together these various formats, you create a richer, more immersive experience for your readers, allowing them to engage with your story on multiple levels and reflect on their own memories in new ways.

Finally, encourage your readers to reflect alongside you. Invite them to pause and consider their own life experiences as they read your reflections. You might pose questions or prompts at the end of certain sections, sparking conversations in the comments or on social media platforms. This interactive approach not only makes your memoir more engaging but also builds a community of individuals who share their reflections and insights. By creating a space for dialogue, you transform your memoir from a solitary endeavor into a collective exploration of memory and meaning in the digital landscape.

06

Chapter 6: Engaging Your Audience

Building a Digital Community

Building a digital community is an essential aspect of crafting a personal narrative in the digital space. As you embark on your journey of memoir writing, consider the power of connection and collaboration with others who share your passion for storytelling and memory preservation. A vibrant digital community not only provides support but also enriches your narrative by exposing you to diverse perspectives and experiences. By engaging with fellow digital fans and storytelling lovers, you can create a network that celebrates the art of memoir writing while fostering personal growth and creativity.

To begin building your digital community, identify platforms that resonate with your interests and goals. Social media sites, writing forums, and blogging platforms offer dynamic spaces where you can share your work, seek feedback, and connect with like-minded individuals. Join online groups or communities dedicated to memoir writing, where you can exchange ideas, ask for advice, and even collaborate on projects. By actively participating in these spaces, you not only gain visibility for your own narrative but also contribute to a collective storytelling process that highlights the unique experiences of all members.

Encourage open dialogue within your community. Sharing your personal stories can inspire others to do the same, creating a ripple effect of vulnerability and authenticity. Consider hosting virtual events such as storytelling nights, webinars, or writing workshops. These gatherings provide opportunities for members to showcase their work and explore different facets of memoir writing. When individuals feel safe and encouraged to share their narratives, the community becomes a nurturing environment where creativity flourishes and connections deepen.

In addition to sharing your own stories, make it a point to engage with the narratives of others. Read their memoirs, comment on their posts, and offer constructive feedback. By investing time in understanding and appreciating the stories of fellow community members, you not only enhance your writing skills but also foster a sense of belonging. This reciprocal relationship builds trust and camaraderie, ensuring that everyone feels valued and supported in their journey of preserving memories and crafting personal narratives.

Finally, remember that building a digital community is an ongoing process. Stay committed to nurturing relationships and expanding your network of digital storytellers. Celebrate the milestones of your peers, share resources, and continue to learn from one another. As you contribute to this vibrant community, you will find that your own storytelling abilities grow stronger, and your personal narrative becomes richer and more compelling. By embracing the power of connection in the digital age, you can create a lasting legacy of memories that resonate with others and contribute to the beautiful tapestry of human experience.

Strategies for Sharing Your Story

Sharing your story in the digital space can be an incredibly rewarding experience, not only for you but also for your audience. To make the most of your narrative, consider starting with authenticity. Your unique voice and perspective are what will resonate with readers. Embrace your experiences, whether they are joyful or challenging; it's this honesty that will forge a connection. Remember, your story is a tapestry woven from the threads of your experiences, and each thread adds depth and richness to your narrative.

Next, leverage the power of multimedia to enhance your storytelling. The digital age offers a myriad of tools that can bring your memories to life in vibrant ways. Incorporate images, videos, or audio clips that complement your written words. These elements can evoke emotions, illustrate key moments, and provide context. For instance, a photograph from a significant event can anchor your narrative in a way that words alone may not achieve. Experiment with different formats, such as blogs, social media posts, or digital scrapbooks, to find the best way to share your story.

Engagement is key when sharing your personal narrative online. Create opportunities for interaction with your audience. This could be through comment sections, social media platforms, or live storytelling events. Ask questions, encourage feedback, and invite your readers to share their own stories. This two-way communication not only fosters a sense of community but also enriches your narrative. When readers feel involved, they are more likely to connect with your story on a personal level and share it with others.

Consider the timing and platforms for sharing your story as well. Different platforms cater to varying audiences and styles of storytelling. Choose spaces that align with your narrative's tone and your personal brand. Whether it's a heartfelt blog post on a personal website or a quick, engaging story on Instagram, ensure you tailor your content to fit the medium. Additionally, timing can influence how your story is received. Share your narrative during moments when it aligns with current events or themes that resonate with your audience for maximum impact.

Finally, don't shy away from vulnerability. Sharing your story means exposing parts of yourself, which can be daunting, but it can also be incredibly liberating. Embrace the imperfections and the lessons learned along the way. Your willingness to be open and vulnerable will inspire others, encouraging them to share their own stories. In a world often filled with curated perfection, your genuine narrative can shine brightly, creating a ripple effect of authenticity and connection among fellow digital fans and storytelling lovers.

Interacting with Readers and Feedback

Interacting with your readers is an essential component of crafting a personal narrative in the digital space. As a memoirist, you are not just sharing your story; you are inviting your audience into your world. This interaction can deepen the connection between you and your readers, enhancing their experience and enriching your narrative. Engaging with your audience through comments, social media, or email can lead to meaningful conversations that provide insight into how your story resonates with others. Embrace this opportunity to listen and learn from the feedback you receive, as it can offer invaluable perspectives on your writing.

Feedback is a powerful tool for growth and improvement. When readers share their thoughts about your memoir, whether they express joy, sadness, or inspiration, it reflects their investment in your story. Take the time to read these comments and consider their viewpoints. You may discover patterns or themes that resonate with your audience, which can guide your future writing endeavors. Constructive criticism can be especially beneficial, as it often highlights areas where you can enhance your narrative clarity or emotional impact. Remember, every piece of feedback is a chance to refine your craft and strengthen your connection with your readers.

Creating a dialogue with your audience can foster a sense of community around your memoir. Consider hosting virtual book clubs or live Q&A sessions where readers can discuss your work and share their own experiences. This not only allows you to connect with your audience on a deeper level but also encourages readers to share their stories. By fostering this environment of openness, you create a space where individuals feel valued and heard, enhancing the overall experience of your memoir. Your readers will appreciate the opportunity to engage directly with you, making them more invested in your journey.

In the digital age, the possibilities for interaction are vast. Utilize social media platforms to share snippets of your writing and invite discussions. Create polls or ask questions to spark engagement and encourage your followers to share their thoughts. You might find that your audience has insights or stories that parallel yours, creating a rich tapestry of shared experiences. This interaction not only broadens your narrative's reach but also enriches it, as the stories of others can provide new layers of meaning to your work.

Ultimately, interacting with readers and embracing feedback is a rewarding aspect of memoir writing in the digital space. It transforms the solitary act of writing into a communal experience, where your story becomes part of a larger narrative that includes the voices and experiences of your audience. As you navigate this journey, remember that every interaction is an opportunity to grow as a writer and to inspire others with your unique memories. Embrace the journey, and let your digital memoir be a catalyst for connection and shared storytelling.

Chapter 7: Preserving Memories

Digital Archives and Their Importance

Digital archives are transforming the way we preserve and share our personal narratives. In a world where memories can easily fade, creating a digital archive allows individuals to capture and maintain their stories in a vibrant and accessible format. These archives serve as a modern scrapbook, enabling us to compile photographs, videos, letters, and other memorabilia into a cohesive narrative that reflects our unique journeys. The significance of digital archives lies not only in their ability to store memories but also in their potential to inspire and connect with others.

One of the most compelling aspects of digital archives is their accessibility. Unlike traditional methods of memory preservation, which can be limited by physical space and the risk of deterioration, digital archives are virtually limitless. You can upload and organize an extensive range of content without worrying about the constraints of a physical medium. This ease of access means that you can revisit your memories anytime, from anywhere, allowing you to relive the moments that matter most. It encourages a deeper engagement with your past, inviting reflection and insight into your personal narrative.

Moreover, digital archives foster creativity and innovation in storytelling. With various tools and platforms available, you can customize your archives to reflect your style and preferences. From interactive timelines to multimedia presentations, the possibilities are endless. This creative freedom empowers you to present your story in a way that resona ez with you and captivates your audience. As digital fans and storytelling lovers, embracing these tools can enhance your memoir writing, making your stories more dynamic and engaging.

In addition to personal benefits, digital archives have the power to build community and connection. Sharing your digital memory collections can inspire others to reflect on their own experiences and narratives. It opens the door to conversations that transcend geograp rizal boundaries, allowing people to connect through shared stories and experiences. By contributing your voice to the digital landscape, you not only preserve your memories but also become part of a broader tapestry of human experience, enriching the lives of those around you.

Finally, the act of creating a digital archive can be profoundly therapeutic. Documenting your memories encourages you to confront and process your past, leading to greater self-awareness and emotional growth. It can serve as a powerful reminder of your resilience and the richness of your experiences. As you craft your personal narrative in the digital space, remember that your story matters. Embrace the importance of digital archives as a tool for preservation, creativity, connection, and healing, and let your memories shine brightly in the ever-evolving digital landscape.

Techniques for Safeguarding Your Work

In the digital age, safeguarding your work is an essential part of the memoir writing journey. With the vast array of tools and platforms available, it's essential to ensure that your personal narratives are protected from loss or unauthorized access. One of the most effective techniques is to regularly back up your work. Cloud storage services like Google Drive, Dropbox, or iCloud offer secure options to store your documents, allowing you to access them from any device. By making it a habit to back up your work frequently, you can rest easy knowing that your memories are safe, even if your device fails.

Another important method for protecting your digital narratives is to use strong passwords and two-factor authentication. Passwords are your first line of defense against unauthorized access to your accounts. Create complex passwords that are difficult to guess and update them regularly. Additionally, enabling two-factor authentication adds an extra layer of security by requiring a second form of verification, such as a text message code or an authentication app. This way, you can safeguard your memoirs against potential breaches and ensure that only you have access to your cherished stories.

Consider also organizing your work into manageable sections and using consistent file naming conventions. This practice not only helps in keeping your projects orderly but also facilitates easier retrieval of your documents when needed. Group your files by themes, dates, or chapters, and adopt a naming system that makes sense to you. Keeping everything organized reduces the risk of losing vital pieces of your narrative and enhances your creative process, allowing you to focus on storytelling rather than searching for lost files.

Moreover, sharing your work selectively with trusted friends or writing groups can provide both feedback and a safety net. When you share your drafts, you not only gain valuable insights but also create a record of your work in the process. Choose platforms that allow you to collaborate but also offer privacy controls, ensuring that your stories remain within your circle until you are ready to publish them. This collaborative approach not only enriches your writing but also reinforces the importance of community support in safeguarding your personal narratives.

Lastly, consider the benefits of creating a physical backup of your work. Printing out your memoirs or keeping a copy on an external hard drive provides a tangible security measure that mitigates the risk of digital loss. While the digital realm is a powerful space for storytelling, having a physical representation of your memories can serve as a comforting reminder of your journey. By employing these techniques, you can confidently navigate the digital landscape, ensuring that your unique stories are preserved for generations to come

Creating a Timeless Digital Legacy

Creating a timeless digital legacy is an empowering journey that allows you to weave your unique story into the fabric of the online world. In an age where memories can easily fade, cultivating a digital presence that reflects your life experiences, values, and aspirations is essential. With the right tools and mindset, you can craft an engaging narrative that resonates with others and stands the test of time. This endeavor is not just about preserving memories; it's about sharing your essence with future generations, ensuring that your voice continues to echo long after you're gone.

Begin by selecting the platforms that resonate with you. Whether it's a personal blog, social media accounts, or dedicated memoir websites, choose spaces that feel comfortable and authentic. Each platform has its strengths; blogs allow for in-depth storytelling, while social media can capture fleeting moments. Embrace the diversity of formats available, from written posts and photo albums to videos and podcasts. This variety not only enriches your narrative but also allows you to express yourself in ways that feel true to your personality.

As you embark on this digital storytelling journey, think about the themes and messages you want to convey. What lessons have shaped your life? What moments are most significant to you? Reflecting on these questions will help you focus your narrative and infuse it with depth. Share the challenges you've faced, the triumphs you've celebrated, and the dreams you still hold. Authenticity is key; readers are drawn to genuine stories that resonate on an emotional level. By being open and honest, you create connections that can inspire and uplift others.

In addition to sharing your own experiences, consider how you can engage with your audience and foster a sense of community. Invite your readers to share their stories, thoughts, and reflections in response to your posts. This interaction not only enriches your narrative but also creates a shared space where memories and experiences can be collectively honored. By building a digital community around your memoir, you create a legacy that includes the voices of others, making it a tapestry of shared human experience.

Finally, remember that creating a digital legacy is a continuous process. Life evolves, and so will your story. Regularly revisit your narrative, update it with new experiences, and reflect on how your perspectives may have changed over time. This practice not only keeps your legacy fresh but also allows you to grow alongside your audience. Embrace the journey of storytelling, and relish the opportunity to leave behind a timeless digital legacy that captures the essence of who you are for generations to come.

08

Chapter 8: Celebrating Your Journey

Acknowledging Growth Through Writing

Acknowledging growth through writing is a powerful experience that can transform not just how we see ourselves but also how we interact with the world around us. In the digital age, where memories can easily be captured and shared at the click of a button, the act of writing becomes a meaningful tool for reflection. Each word we type serves as a stepping stone on our personal journeys, allowing us to track our evolution over time. Embracing this process encourages us to recognize our progress, celebrate our achievements, and learn from our challenges.

As you craft your personal narrative, consider how your writing can serve as a mirror. It reflects not only who you are today but also who you were at various points in your life. By revisiting past entries, you may find that your perspective has shifted or that your understanding of certain events has deepened. This acknowledgment of growth fosters a sense of gratitude for the experiences that have shaped you. With each memory documented, you create a tapestry of resilience, reminding yourself that every challenge faced has contributed to your development.

Digital platforms provide an accessible and dynamic way to share your story with others. This sharing is not just about seeking validation; it's an opportunity to connect with like-minded individuals who are also on their journeys of self-discovery. When you open up about your experiences, you invite others to do the same, creating a sense of community rooted in mutual understanding and support. Your words can resonate with someone who may be going through similar struggles, reinforcing the idea that we are all interconnected through our narratives.

Embracing growth through writing can also enhance your storytelling skills. As you reflect on your past, you may discover new angles and insights that enrich your narrative. This evolution of thought can lead to more profound storytelling, allowing you to engage your audience on a deeper level. Writing becomes not just a record of your experiences but an art form that continues to develop alongside you. With each piece you create, you hone your craft, fostering a sense of pride in your ability to articulate your journey.

Finally, acknowledging growth through writing is a celebration of your resilience and creativity. It is an affirmation that you are a work in progress, and that's perfectly okay. As you document your memories online, remember to honor the journey itself. Each entry is a testament to your willingness to reflect, evolve, and share your truth with the world. Embrace this process with open arms, and allow your writing to be a beacon of hope and inspiration, not only for yourself but for all who encounter your e-memories.

Sharing Your Work with Confidence

Sharing your work with confidence is a crucial step in the journey of crafting your personal narrative, especially in the digital space. As you embark on this path, remember that your story is unique and valuable. Embracing the courage to share your experiences not only enriches your own narrative but also connects you with others who may resonate with your journey. Each word you write has the potential to inspire, heal, and create community, reminding you that your voice matters.

To build your confidence, start by recognizing the importance of vulnerability in storytelling. When you share your thoughts and experiences, you invite others into your world, allowing them to see the beauty and complexity of your life. Understand that many readers appreciate authenticity over perfection. As you write, let your true self shine through. Share the highs and lows, the laughter and the tears, allowing your audience to connect with the real you. This authenticity will help foster a sense of trust and engagement with your readers.

As you prepare to share your work, consider the platforms available to you. The digital landscape is vast, offering numerous avenues for expression, from personal blogs to social media and online writing communities. Explore these options and choose the ones that resonate most with you. Tailor your approach to each platform, understanding that some may be more suited for longer narratives while others thrive on short, impactful snippets. Embrace the diversity of these platforms as opportunities to reach different audiences and share your story in varied formats.

Feedback can be an invaluable tool as you share your work. Seek out supportive communities of fellow writers and storytelling enthusiasts who can provide constructive criticism and encouragement. Engage with your audience through comments and messages, appreciating their insights and perspectives. Remember that not all feedback will resonate with you, and that's okay. Use it as a learning opportunity, and trust your instincts about the direction you want your narrative to take. This ongoing dialogue can deepen your confidence and refine your storytelling skills.

Ultimately, sharing your work is about more than just putting words on a screen; it's about creating connections and fostering a sense of belonging. Each time you share your story, you contribute to a larger tapestry of human experience. Embrace the journey of sharing your narrative with confidence, knowing that you have the power to touch lives and inspire others. Your story is not just yours; it belongs to everyone who finds solace, strength, or inspiration within its pages.

Continuing Your Story Beyond the Page

Continuing your story beyond the page means embracing the limitless potential of digital platforms to share your memoir. In today's interconnected world, your personal narrative can extend far beyond the confines of a printed book. Imagine your experiences not only read as text but also shared through multimedia, engaging your audience in ways that traditional storytelling cannot. By utilizing blogs, social media, or even podcasting, you can create an immersive experience that brings your memories to life and invites others to join in your journey.

As you transition your narrative into the digital realm, think about the various forms your story can take. Video diaries, interactive timelines, or photo essays can enhance your memoir and offer unique perspectives on your experiences. These tools allow you to showcase your personality and creativity while connecting with a broader audience. Remember, your story is not just a series of events; it's a tapestry of emotions, lessons, and insights. By exploring different media, you can highlight the richness of your narrative and foster deeper connections with your readers.

Engaging with your audience is a vital aspect of continuing your story. The digital space provides opportunities for interaction that were previously unavailable. Encourage feedback, invite questions, and create forums for discussions about your experiences. This engagement can transform your memoir into a collaborative journey, where readers feel they are part of your story. They can share their own experiences, offer insights, or simply express how your narrative resonated with them. This connection not only enriches your storytelling but also builds a community around shared experiences.

Moreover, consider the potential for serialized storytelling in the digital landscape. Instead of sharing your entire memoir at once, you can release chapters or segments over time. This method keeps your audience engaged and eagerly anticipating the next installment of your story. It also allows for real-time feedback and adaptation, letting you refine your narrative based on readers' reactions. By maintaining this ongoing dialogue, you foster a sense of intimacy and connection, making your audience feel invested in your journey.

Finally, don't forget to revisit and update your story as your life evolves. Digital memoirs are not static; they can grow and change as you do. Share new insights, experiences, or lessons learned along the way. This dynamic aspect of digital storytelling allows your narrative to remain relevant and reflective of your current self. By continuing to share your journey, you not only honor your past but also inspire others to embrace their own evolving stories. Your memoir, both online and offline, becomes a living testament to the power of personal narratives in the digital age.

09

Chapter 9: Looking Ahead

The Future of Memoir Writing in the Digital Age

The future of memoir writing in the digital age is filled with exciting possibilities that empower individuals to share their stories like never before. With the rise of social media, blogs, and digital storytelling platforms, anyone with a passion for storytelling can carve out their space in the vast landscape of the internet. This democratization of memoir writing allows voices from all walks of life to contribute to the collective narrative, creating a rich tapestry of experiences that resonate with diverse audiences. Embrace this opportunity; your story matters and deserves to be told.

As technology continues to evolve, so do the tools available for memoir writers. From use-friendly writing apps to multimedia platforms that allow for the integration of photos, videos, and audio, the digital realm offers endless ways to enhance personal narratives. Imagine weaving your written words with visual and auditory elements, creating a more immersive experience for your readers. These innovations not only enhance storytelling but also make it more accessible, allowing writers to connect with others across the globe, fostering a sense of community among those who share similar experiences.

Moreover, the digital age encourages collaboration and interaction between writers and their audiences. Readers can now engage with memoirs through comments, shares, and discussions, creating a dialogue that enriches the storytelling experience. This feedback loop can be incredibly motivating for writers, as they see the impact of their narratives on others. It's a chance to build relationships around shared experiences, helping to normalize and validate the myriad of emotions and challenges we all face. Your memoir can inspire, heal, and connect people in ways that traditional formats may not.

The future also holds tremendous potential for the preservation and archiving of personal narratives. Digital platforms allow for the easy storage and organization of memories, ensuring that your story remains accessible for generations to come. With the possibility of creating digital scrapbooks or interactive timelines, memoir writing can transcend the limitations of paper and traditional publishing. Imagine your grandchildren exploring your life story through a dynamic digital format that brings your memories to life, allowing them to understand your experiences in context.

Ultimately, the digital age invites you to embrace your unique voice and share your memoir with the world. Whether you're writing for yourself, your family, or a broader audience, the tools and platforms available today make it easier than ever to craft and share your narrative. Don't hesitate to explore the various avenues for storytelling that await you. The future of memoir writing is bright, and by stepping into this digital space, you can leave a lasting legacy that inspires others and preserves your memories for years to come.

Evolving with Technology

In the rapidly changing landscape of technology, the art of storytelling has found new avenues for expression. As digital fans and storytelling enthusiasts, you have the unique opportunity to embrace these advancements and enhance your memoir writing. The advent of online platforms, social media, and multimedia tools allows you to craft rich, immersive narratives that resonate with a global audience. By leveraging these technologies, you can not only document your personal experiences but also share them in innovative ways that engage and inspire others.

Consider how digital platforms enable you to curate your memories with greater flexibility. Instead of relying solely on written text, you can incorporate images, audio, and video into your memoir. This multi-faceted approach adds depth to your stories, allowing your audience to connect with your experiences on various levels. Imagine sharing a cherished family moment through a short video clip or enhancing a poignant passage with an evocative photograph. These elements can transform simple narratives into vivid, engaging experiences that captivate your readers.

Moreover, the rise of social media has democratized storytelling, allowing you to reach diverse audiences and connect with fellow memoirists. Platforms like Instagram, TikTok, and blog sites provide spaces to share snippets of your narrative, receive feedback, and engage in meaningful conversations. This interaction not only enriches your storytelling but also fosters a supportive community of like-minded individuals who share your passion for preserving memories. Engaging with this community can spark new ideas and inspire you to push the boundaries of your narrative craft.

As you navigate the digital landscape, remember that technology is a tool to enhance your voice, not a replacement for it. Your unique perspective and personal experiences remain at the core of your memoir. Embrace the technological innovations available, but allow your authentic voice to shine through. Whether you choose to write a traditional blog, create a multimedia project, or share your journey on social media, stay true to the essence of your story. This authenticity will resonate with your audience, creating connections that transcend the digital realm.

In this age of digital storytelling, the possibilities are endless. You are not just chronicling your life; you are crafting a legacy that can inspire future generations. Embrace the evolving technology around you, harness its potential, and let your creativity flourish. Your memories deserve to be celebrated, and with the right tools at your fingertips, you can ensure they are shared in ways that honor their significance. The journey of memoir writing in the digital age is not just about preserving the past; it is about shaping the future of storytelling.

Inspiring the Next Generation of Storytellers

In a world where stories can be shared with just a click, the next generation of storyteller stands on the brink of digital creativity. The power of technology has made storytelling more accessible than ever before, inviting young voices to express their unique experiences and perspectives. By harnessing digital platforms, aspiring memoirists can craft their narratives in compelling ways that resonate with diverse audiences. Encouraging this new wave of storytellers not only enriches the literary landscape but also empowers individuals to connect with their own histories and those of others.

The essence of storytelling lies in its ability to evoke emotions and foster connections. As digital fans and lovers of storytelling, we have a responsibility to nurture the talents of emerging writers. By sharing our own experiences and offering constructive feedback, we can create an encouraging environment that inspires them to explore their creativity. Engaging in workshops, online forums, or even social media groups dedicated to memoir writing can provide invaluable support, helping young storytellers refine their craft while celebrating their unique voices.

Digital platforms also offer innovative ways to tell stories that were previously unimaginable. With the integration of multimedia elements like video, audio, and interactive graphics, memoirists can enhance their narratives and captivate their audience's attention. Encouraging young writers to experiment with these tools can lead to exciting new forms of storytelling that combine traditional writing with modern technology. By exploring these avenues, the next generation can create immersive experiences that leave a lasting impact on their readers.

Moreover, promoting inclusivity in storytelling is vital for the growth of a diverse literary community. By encouraging young storytellers from various backgrounds to share their experiences, we can foster a richer tapestry of narratives that reflect the complexities of our world. This diversity not only enriches the storytelling landscape but also ensures that all voices are heard. As mentors and supporters, we can advocate for marginalized voices by providing platforms and resources that empower them to tell their stories authentically.

Inspiring the next generation of storytellers is a collective effort that requires passion, patience, and dedication. By fostering a culture of encouragement, sharing resources, and championing diversity, we can help young writers navigate the digital landscape of memoir writing. As they embrace the tools and technologies at their disposal, we can look forward to a future filled with captivating stories that not only preserve memories but also inspire change and understanding in an ever-evolving world.

From Memory to Memoir: Embracing the Digital Canvas

Thank you for exploring this book on digital memoir writing. In our increasingly connected world, our stories transcend mere records to become valuable legacies that bridge past and future. "E-Memories: Crafting a Personal Narrative in the Digital Space" serves as your guide to expressing memories and experiences richly in the digital realm. From Chapter 1 through Chapter 9, we journey from the fundamentals of storytelling to finding your authentic voice, selecting appropriate platforms, structuring your memoir, and engaging with your audience. Digital memoir writing represents more than self-expression—it creates empathy and connection. Your story has the power to inspire and encourage others. While technology continually evolves, the value of an authentic voice remains constant. I encourage you to share your unique experiences, emotions, and insights fearlessly. I hope this book becomes a trusted companion on your digital storytelling journey and helps nurture the next generation of storytellers. Each personal narrative contributes to the rich tapestry we collectively weave in the digital space.

Professor Hiroko Oe
BA in Economics, University of Tokyo
MSc in Regulation, London School of Economics
PhD in Information and Communication Studies, Waseda University
Professor, Josai International University
Former Professor, Bournemouth University Graduate School, UK